EARTH'S CYCLES
IN ACTION

EARTH'S CYCLES

By Diane Dakers

CRABTREE
Publishing Company
www.crabtreebooks.com

Crabtree Publishing Company
www.crabtreebooks.com

Author: Diane Dakers
Publishing plan research and development:
   Reagan Miller
Project coordinator: Mark Sachner,
   Water Buffalo Books
Editors: Mark Sachner, Shirley Duke
Proofreader: Shannon Welbourn
Editorial director: Kathy Middleton
Photo researcher: Ruth Owen
Designer: Westgraphix/Tammy West
Contributing writer and indexer: Suzy Gazlay
Production coordinator
   and prepress technician: Margaret Amy Salter
Print coordinator: Katherine Berti
Science, reading, and curriculum consultant:
Suzy Gazlay, M.A.; Recipient, Presidential Award for
Excellence in Science Teaching

Written, developed, and produced by
Water Buffalo Books

Photographs and reproductions:
Front Cover: Shutterstock: Eduardo Rivero
(Background); Reddogs: (Geese)

Interior: Alamy: pp. 18, 27. **FLPA:** pp. 17, 39 **NASA:**
pp. 8, 9 (right), 13, 29, 30, 37 (top), 41. Gregory H.
Revera: p. 20 **Ruby Tuesday Books Ltd:** pp. 10, 25, 26.
Science Photo Library: pp. 16, 31, 34, 35.
Shutterstock: pp. 1, 3, 4, 5, 6, 9 (left), 11, 12, 14, 15
(left), 18 (bottom), 19, 21, 23, 24, 27 (bottom), 32, 33,
36, 37 (bottom), 38, 40, 42, 43, 44, 45, 47.
Shutterstock: kmichal: p. 15 (right).

Library and Archives Canada Cataloguing in Publication

Dakers, Diane, author
   Earth's cycles / Diane Dakers.

(Earth's cycles in action)
Includes index.
Issued in print and electronic formats.
ISBN 978-0-7787-0640-3 (bound).--
ISBN 978-0-7787-0619-9 (pbk.).--
ISBN 978-1-4271-7624-0 (pdf).--ISBN 978-1-4271-7620-2 (html)

   1. Earth sciences--Juvenile literature. 2. Earth (Planet)--
Juvenile literature. I. Title.

QE29.D35 2014   j550   C2014-903928-X
                                     C2014-903929-8

Library of Congress Cataloging-in-Publication Data

Dakers, Diane, author.
 Earth's cycles / Diane Dakers.
      pages cm. -- (Earth's cycles in action)
 Includes index.
 ISBN 978-0-7787-0640-3 (reinforced library binding) --
ISBN 978-0-7787-0619-9 (pbk.) --
ISBN 978-1-4271-7624-0 (electronic pdf) --
ISBN 978-1-4271-7620-2 (electronic html)
 1. Earth sciences--Juvenile literature. 2. Earth (Planet)--
Juvenile literature. I. Title.

 QE29.D324 2015
 550--dc23
                         2014032597

Crabtree Publishing Company
www.crabtreebooks.com   1-800-387-7650

Printed in Canada/102014/EF20140925

**Published
in Canada
Crabtree Publishing**
616 Welland Ave.
St. Catharines, Ontario
L2M 5V6

**Published in
the United States
Crabtree Publishing**
PMB 59051
350 Fifth Ave., 59th Floor
New York, NY 10118

**Published in the
United Kingdom
Crabtree Publishing**
Maritime House
Basin Road North, Hove
BN41 1WR

**Published
in Australia
Crabtree Publishing**
3 Charles Street
Coburg North
VIC, 3058

Contents

Climate zones

Polar Zones

El Niño

Tidal bulge

Troposphere

CHAPTER 1

Cycles Make the World Go 'Round

A frog lays a mass of eggs. Before long, the eggs hatch and become tadpoles. The tadpoles grow legs and become froglets. Eventually, the froglets become full-grown adult frogs, which lay eggs of their own. These new eggs hatch into tadpoles, which become froglets that grow into adult frogs, which lay eggs ... and so on. This is an example of a cycle, a pattern of related processes or events that happen over and over again. Like a circle, a cycle has no beginning and ending. It just keeps going and going and going...

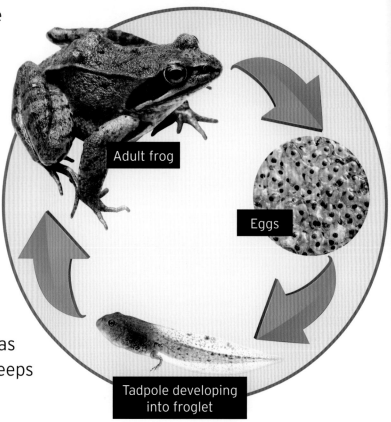

Adult frog

Eggs

Tadpole developing into froglet

Cycles of Life

Every day, Earth is filled with many cycles. In fact, every day is a cycle, which we divide into units of hours, minutes, and seconds. These units of the clock help us measure our time within the daily cycle as we go to school, relax and do homework, and sleep at night. Then, in the morning, we awaken and rejoin the daily cycle!

Many cycles happen so regularly and constantly that we don't even think about them. The passing seasons, the phases of the Moon, rising and falling tides—these are all connected to the Sun's energy and gravity, and to Earth's place in the solar system. They are never-ending patterns that affect the lives of all living things.

Sun and Moon

Every day, Earth rotates, or spins, on its axis, creating day and night. Every year, Earth makes one full trip, or orbit, around the Sun. At different times of year, different parts of Earth are tilted more toward the Sun and receive more direct sunlight than other parts of Earth. Seasons come and go.

Meanwhile, the Moon orbits Earth about once a month. It sometimes shines as a bright full Moon, and sometimes it appears nearly completely dark and invisible without the aid of a telescope.

All these cycles have been happening for as long as our planet and its Moon have existed, and they affect life on Earth every day. Humans can't change how these cycles happen, but if we understand how they work, we can better control how they affect us and other living things. For example, we use our knowledge of Earth's cycles to predict the weather. We also use our understanding of these cycles to figure out when to plant crops. We now use sunlight and the rising and falling of ocean tides to generate energy. In these ways, we have begun to harness the power of the Sun and the Moon to provide new forms of energy for life here on Earth!

The Sun shining brightly by day, and the Moon reflecting the Sun's light by night, are reminders of our planet's relationship with other bodies in space. They are also a part of daily, monthly, and yearly cycles that help shape our lives on Earth.

CHAPTER 2

You Are Here

In the late 1990s, TV viewers were entertained by a comedy called *3rd Rock from the Sun*. The show was about aliens from another planet living on Earth. The aliens thought Earth was a boring place, nothing more than, well, the third rock from the Sun! They were right about a couple of things. It's true that Earth has a hard, rocky surface, although that surface is largely covered with water. It's also true that Earth is the third rocky planet from the Sun. Mercury is the closest "rock" to the Sun, followed by Venus, then Earth and Mars. The aliens on that TV show were wrong, though, about Earth being a dull place. We know this planet is extra-special, because it's the only one in this solar system that we know for sure can support life.

Both Earth and its Moon are rocky objects in space. Earth, however, has water, an **atmosphere**, and all the other ingredients to support the incredible variety of life on our planet.

Life Support

Earth is part of a system called a solar system. Scientists believe our solar system was created 4.5 billion years ago. It is made up of eight planets that circle, or orbit, the Sun, each staying in its own path. In order, from closest to the Sun, are the planets Mercury, Venus, Earth, Mars, Jupiter, Saturn, Uranus, and Neptune. Between Mars and Jupiter is the **asteroid** belt. This is a ring of rocky bodies, or asteroids, left over from the creation of the solar system. There are millions of asteroids in the solar system, and most of them are here. Beyond Neptune is another donut-shaped area in space. It is called the **Kuiper Belt**, and it extends for billions of miles beyond Neptune's orbit. It is filled with millions of icy objects and comets held in orbit by the Sun's gravity. Surrounding this

MAKING SENSE OF CYCLES

Many cycles on our planet, like that of a frog's life, take place in ways that we can observe. In what we call the water cycle, for example, we see and feel the effects of rain, snow, water freezing, ice melting, evaporation, and even clouds in the sky. But we also need microscopes or other special equipment to see everything that is going on. Do any of the cycles discussed so far in this book affect your own life? Why or why not? Using examples from this book and your own life, keep a list of cycles that can happen in your body and in the environment around you. How do these cycles affect you? What would happen if any of these cycles were broken or interrupted?

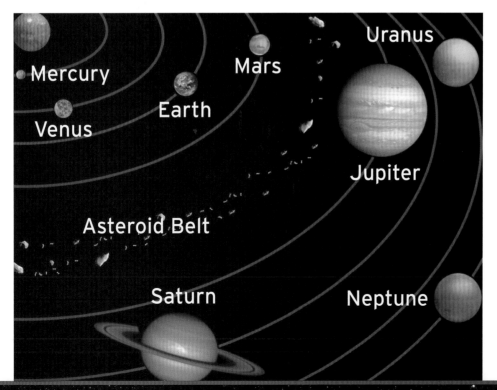

Mercury

Venus

Earth

Mars

Uranus

Jupiter

Asteroid Belt

Saturn

Neptune

This diagram shows the positions of the planets and asteroid belt in our solar system as they travel around the Sun. The sizes and distances are not shown to scale in this composite photo image.

Heavenly Bodies

The planets and the bodies in the asteroid belt aren't the only objects in our solar system. Most planets, including Earth, also have moons. Earth has one. Mars has two. Astronomers have identified at least 146 moons orbiting Jupiter and Saturn combined and are working to confirm nearly 30 more! The only planets without moons are Mercury and Venus. Other bodies in the solar system include comets, asteroids outside the asteroid belt, and other bits of rock, gas, and dust.

Also present in the solar system are objects that fall somewhere between the size of asteroids and planets. The best known of these, Pluto, was discovered in 1930 and classified as the ninth planet in our solar system. In 2005, however, a larger orbiting object, named Eris, was discovered. In 2006, new astronomical standards led to Pluto no longer being classified as a planet. Its status was changed to dwarf planet that year.

Our solar system is part of a galaxy called the Milky Way. Scientists believe that the Milky Way contains up to 400 billion stars, including our Sun, and that about 100 billion other planets orbit those stars.

whole system is another, even larger area called the **Oort Cloud**. This is a sphere-shaped region that extends almost 2,000 times farther out into space than the Kuiper Belt. The Oort Cloud may contain more than a trillion icy bodies of different sizes.

Of the planets in the solar system, Jupiter is the largest. Mercury is the smallest. Earth is the fourth smallest, and it's the only planet that is home to plants, animals, and other living organisms that thrive on our planet. That's because Earth has liquid water and a temperature just right for supporting life.

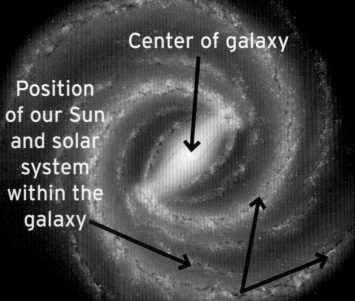

Center of galaxy

Position of our Sun and solar system within the galaxy

Spiral arms of the galaxy made up of stars

This art shows our galaxy, the Milky Way, as if seen from above. If you could travel at the speed of light, which is about 186,282 miles (300,000 kilometers) per second, it would take you 100,000 years to get from one end to the other!

Earth is also the right distance from the Sun to receive just enough, but not too much, heat and light from the Sun. Venus, for example, is too close to the Sun to support life. It is so hot on Venus that water would boil away, and plants and animals would burn to death. Mars, on the other hand, is too far from the Sun. Any water on that planet is frozen under polar ice caps. It is so cold on Mars that no living thing we know of could survive there.

On Earth, the Sun's energy provides just the right amount of heat for water to exist mostly in a liquid state.

All plants and animals need water to survive.

The Sun's energy also powers a process in plants called **photosynthesis**. In this process, plants take in water from the soil and carbon dioxide from the atmosphere. Using energy from the Sun, they convert these substances into sugars and oxygen. The sugars feed the plants, and the oxygen is released into the air. That oxygen is what nearly all of Earth's animals depend on to stay alive.

Surface of Earth

Surface of Mars

These two photos offer a striking contrast between conditions on Earth (left) and its planetary neighbor Mars (right), as photographed by cameras on the Pathfinder mission in 1997. One key to the conditions that make possible this life-sustaining waterfall scene is Earth's "just-right" distance from the Sun.

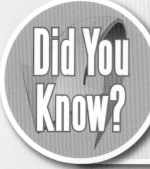

Like our planet, the Moon also spins on its axis as it moves through its orbit around Earth. One fascinating thing about the Moon is that one full rotation on its axis takes the same amount of time as one full orbit around Earth. This means that the same side of the Moon always faces Earth, and the Moon rotates one full turn every time it travels once around Earth.

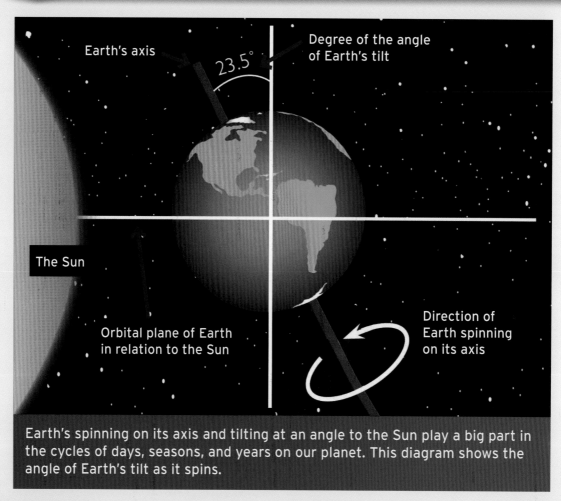

Earth's axis

23.5°

Degree of the angle of Earth's tilt

The Sun

Orbital plane of Earth in relation to the Sun

Direction of Earth spinning on its axis

Earth's spinning on its axis and tilting at an angle to the Sun play a big part in the cycles of days, seasons, and years on our planet. This diagram shows the angle of Earth's tilt as it spins.

Tilt and Spin

While Earth travels in its orbit around the Sun, it is also spinning on its **axis**. The axis is an imaginary line that runs through Earth, from the North to the South Poles. Earth makes one full rotation on its axis every 23 hours and 56 minutes. We call that a day, and we round it up to 24 hours. As our planet spins on

its axis, we experience daytime and nighttime. The way Earth is tilted on its axis, along with its position in its path around the Sun, also determines how much light different parts of the planet receive at different times of the year.

The equator is an imaginary line that circles the middle of Earth like a

Earthly Facts

- Earth is about 93 million miles (150 million km) from the Sun.
- Earth weighs about 6,600 billion tons.
- Earth isn't completely round. It's a bit wider around the equator than it is through the North and South Poles.
- Earth's center is made of liquid rock that is slightly hotter than the surface of the Sun!
- Earth travels around the Sun at about 67,000 miles (107,826 km) per hour.
- About 70 percent of Earth's surface is covered with water.

belt. For places near the equator, the amount of sunshine doesn't change much from day to day, or month to month. Places to the north and south of the equator, though, experience different amounts of sunshine at different times of the year.

Whether it's night or day, winter or summer, the Sun plays the most important role in the existence of our planet. Let's take a closer look at the cycles of Earth, and how the Sun impacts life on this rock of ours.

A photo album showcasing the variety of habitats and climates teeming with life on Earth. From left: A subtropical desert in the Southwestern United States; a tropical rain forest near the equator in Southeast Asia; dolphins playing beneath the surface of the ocean; and a penguin colony near an iceberg in Antarctica.

CHAPTER 3

Sunrise, Sunset, Seasons

Scientists believe that the Milky Way is one of more than 100 billion galaxies in the known universe. Based on estimates of hundreds of billions of stars in each galaxy, this makes the Sun one of an estimated 300 *sextillion* stars in the known universe. Using numerals, that figure looks like this: 300,000,000,000,000,000,000,000!

Of all those stars, the Sun just happens to be *our* star—the one that brings Earth to life! Because it is so important to human survival, ancient peoples worshipped the Sun. They believed the Sun was a god, and they wanted to keep that god happy. In some countries, they held ceremonies to honor the Sun. They danced, sang, and made offerings to the Sun. The idea was to encourage this great god to bring good weather and healthy crops to the people. Today, we know a lot more about the Sun, its relation to Earth, and its importance to life on Earth.

Ancient peoples worshipped the Sun in the hope that it would bring good weather and healthy crops. We still appreciate our star for those same gifts today!

Spotlight on the Sun

The Sun is huge. It is more than a million times the size of Earth—and Earth is already pretty big! It would take 109 Earths, laid side-by-side, just to make a single line across the face of the Sun. The Sun is so big that it contains 99.9 percent of the total mass of the entire solar system. The remaining 0.1 percent is made up of all the planets, moons, asteroids, comets, dust, and gas in the solar system combined.

It's no wonder that this star has so much influence on Earth!

Sun Signs

- The Sun weighs 333,000 times as much as Earth. About 960,000 Earths could fit inside the Sun.
- Light from the Sun travels at a speed of about 186,282 miles (300,000 km) per second and takes about eight minutes to reach Earth.
- A passenger jet cruising at a speed of around 550 miles per hour (885 kmh) would take about 19 years to fly from Earth to the Sun.
- The core of the Sun is the hottest place in the solar system, with temperatures as high as 27 million degrees Fahrenheit (15 million degrees Celsius).
- The surface of the Sun is much cooler—a relatively chilly temperature of about 10,000°F (5,500°C). That's 100 times hotter than the hottest temperature ever recorded on Earth.

Earth

Sun

Earth is almost 8,000 miles (12,800 km) wide. The Sun, on the other hand, is 865,374 miles (1,392,684 km) wide. In these photos, in which the sizes but not the distances are shown to scale, Earth looks like a tiny dot by comparison!

What Shape Your Shadow Is In

Earth's rotation changes the shape of your shadow. If you stand in the bright sunshine in the early morning, with the Sun appearing far to the east, your shadow makes a long, lean shape on the ground to the west of where you're standing. Later in the morning, due to Earth's rotation the Sun appears higher in the sky, and your shadow gets shorter and stockier, but it still falls to the west. At high noon, you have almost no shadow. That's because as Earth continues to rotate, the Sun appears directly over your head, and your shadow is directly beneath you at this point! After noon, as the Sun appears to move to the west, your shadow moves to the east. It gets longer and longer until late afternoon, as the Sun is setting. At that point, your shadow is a long, lean shape to the east—exactly the opposite of where it started in the morning!

The Sun's massive gravity holds Earth and all the planets in orbit. The Sun also influences weather patterns and **climate zones** on Earth. It gives us both the seasons and day and night.

We know that every 24 hours, Earth makes one full rotation on its axis. When the place where you live faces the Sun, you have daylight. When it faces away, you're in the dark of night.

During the day, the spinning of Earth makes it appear that the Sun rises and sets and moves from east to west across the sky. It also appears, at night, that the stars travel through the sky. We know that the Sun and the stars don't actually move in relation to Earth. It is our planet, and us with it, that are moving. Earth's rotation makes it look like the Sun and other stars are traveling through the sky. There was a time, though, up until about 350 years ago, that people thought it was the other way around. They thought that Earth stood still and the Sun moved around where the Sun appears in the sky.

It isn't just Earth's rotation on its axis that changes the Sun's position in the sky. Earth's tilt and orbit also change where the Sun appears to be above us.

Earth always tilts in the same direction. This means that, as it travels around the Sun, it sometimes tilts toward the Sun, and sometimes it tilts away from the Sun.

Because of the tilt of Earth's axis, the Sun appears at different heights in the sky at different times of the year. Left: The Sun appears high in the sky over this summer scene. Right: The Sun appears lower in the sky, and farther to the south, over these skaters in New York City in the middle of winter.

If you live in the northern **hemisphere**, the Sun is tilted more toward the Sun during late June, July, August, and early September. That means places north of the equator are closer to the Sun, and warmer, at that time of year. At the same time, the Sun also appears to climb higher in the sky and the days are longer. This is summertime in the northern hemisphere.

Summer in the southern hemisphere happens from mid December to mid March. That's when the northern portion of Earth is tilted *away* from the Sun. This means that points south of the equator are closer to the Sun at that time. When the days are long, and the Sun is high in the sky in the south, the northern part of Earth experiences shorter, colder days—winter.

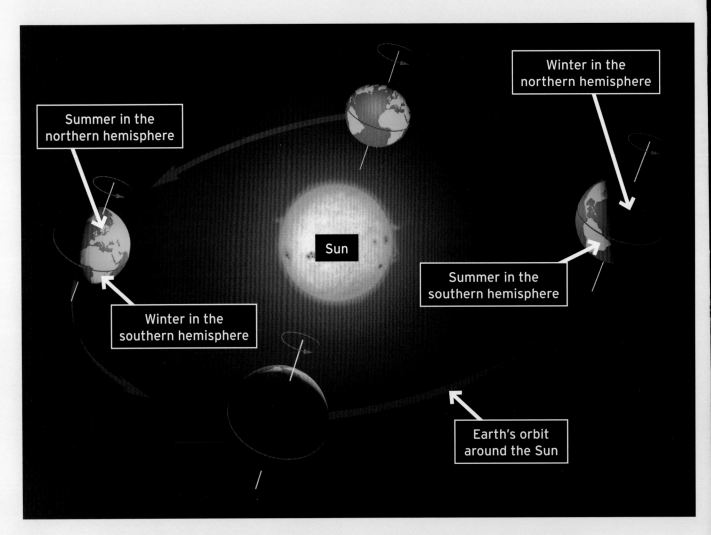

As Earth orbits the Sun, it always tilts in the same direction. This diagram shows how that tilt places some parts of the planet more in direct sunlight at certain times of the year, and less at others. The angle of Earth's tilt thus affects the seasons as we and our planet travel around the Sun.

In both hemispheres, when Earth is between summer and winter, it is autumn. The hours of daylight and darkness on our planet are never exactly the same, but they become more "equal" at this time of year. The same thing happens in spring, when Earth is between winter and summer.

Zoning Out on Earth

Every part of Earth actually has different seasons, but in some places, it doesn't feel that way. Different parts of the planet are in different climate zones.

The North and South Poles, for example, are in the **polar zone**. There, it is dry and ice-covered all year-round. It's also freezing cold all year-round. That's because the Sun's rays always strike these polar zones at an angle. The light there is indirect, or less focused, than the sunlight that reaches other parts of the planet. This indirect sunlight is also cooler than the direct light that strikes Earth at the equator, for example. So even though there are changes in temperature between summer and winter in the polar zones, you can be sure it's always cold!

Although the tilt of Earth's axis assures that it's cold in the polar regions all year-round, changes in temperature allow for seasonal activities. Above: paddling a kayak near an Arctic glacier in July!

In terms of sunlight in those two regions, however, there are two dramatically different seasons. At the North Pole, in the summer months, the Sun is above the horizon and shines 24 hours a day. That's because the pole is pointed more toward the Sun. On the other hand, during the winter, the Sun is below the horizon and doesn't rise for weeks on end. That's when the North Pole is tilted away from the Sun, and it's in the shadows. The same thing happens at the South Pole at opposite times of year—when it's winter at the North Pole, it's summer at the South Pole.

As you travel away from the poles, toward the equator, you pass through another climate zone. This one is called the **temperate zone**, and it includes nearly all of the United States, most of Canada, plus Europe, northern Asia, and the southern part of South America.

In the northern hemisphere, the longest day of the year is in June. In this time-lapse photo, taken in Alaska around that time, we see the occurrence known as "the midnight Sun." The Sun remains visible in the night sky even at the point where it comes closest to "setting." As the diagram (inset) shows, at this time the entire region around the North Pole is entirely in sunlight, and the region around the South Pole is in darkness.

N — Polar day

Polar night   S

People in the temperate zone experience four clear seasons, with noticeably different temperatures and weather conditions in each season.

Places in the world that are nearer the equator are in the **tropical zone**. Here, the Sun is closest to Earth and shines most directly on Earth all year long, and it is hot all year-round. Still, there are two distinct seasons—a rainy season and a dry season.

Energy from the Sun drives cycles of wind and **air pressure** that determine when the wet and dry seasons occur each year. In the tropical zone south of the equator, the rainy season takes place from October to March. North of the equator, the rainy season happens from April to September.

Day and night, seasons, weather, and climate—all these cycles are connected to Earth's relationship with the Sun. And this relationship is connected to two very important cycles—our planet's rotation on its axis and its orbital path around the Sun. Meanwhile, the Moon is responsible for some Earthly cycles of its own.

Typically, in a temperate climate zone, plants sprout in spring. In summer, they grow leaves, flowers, and fruit. In autumn, plants drop seeds and many trees drop their leaves. In winter, plants rest and many die off completely.

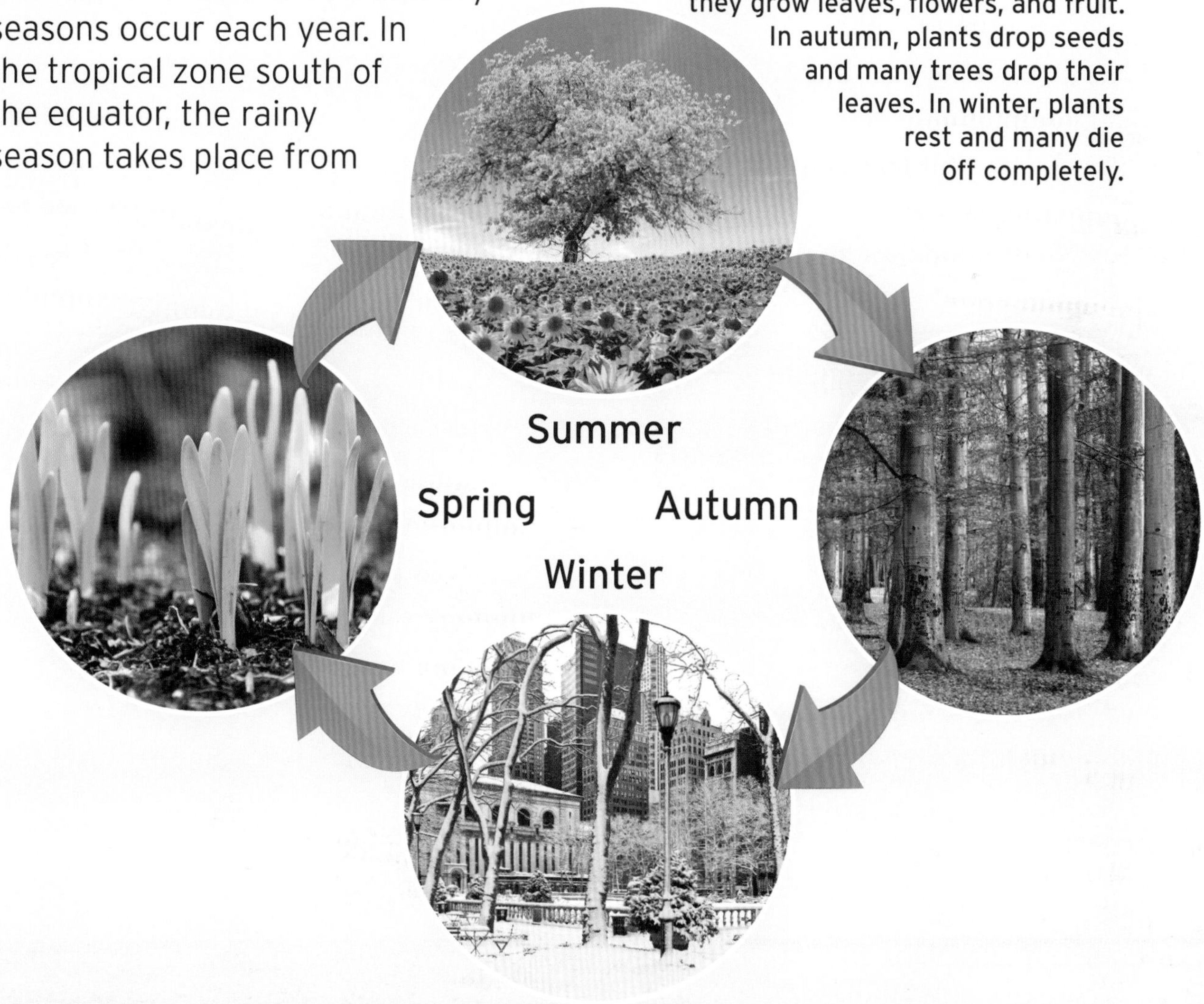

Summer

Spring   Autumn

Winter

Just as some ancient cultures worshipped the Sun, many also worshipped the Moon. Some ancient peoples believed the Moon was a god, goddess, or spirit sent to help them or protect them. Because it is the largest and brightest object in the night sky, the Moon has also inspired many myths and legends. It is often connected with motherhood, wisdom, birth, death, the afterlife—and madness. The word "lunatic," to describe a person who is mentally ill, comes from Luna, the name of the Roman goddess of the Moon. Even today, some people believe a full moon makes humans do strange things. According to some legends, they might even turn into werewolves!

The Moon has been Earth's companion in space for about 4.5 billion years. This photograph shows the face of the Moon as seen from Earth's northern hemisphere.

Phasing In and Out

Without the Sun, we would not see the Moon. The Moon does not give off its own light. Instead, it reflects the light of the Sun back to Earth. Sometimes the Moon appears as a full circle in the sky. That's called a full moon, and it happens when the Moon is positioned so the Sun lights up the entire face of the Moon as we see it from Earth.

The full moon appears in the night sky every 29.5 days. This time period—from full moon to full moon—is called a lunar cycle, or **lunar month**. The lunar month isn't quite the same as a calendar month. Sometimes, in fact, there are two full moons in one calendar month, one at the beginning of the month, the other at the end. This is called a **blue moon**, even though it's not blue! In some traditions, full moons were often given names, such as "Pink" or "Strawberry," depending on when they occurred. "Blue" happened to be the name given to the place in the cycle of full moons when this "extra" full moon occurred. It also gave birth to the expression "once in a blue moon" to describe any event that rarely happens!

As Earth orbits the Sun and the Moon orbits Earth during a lunar month, the Moon appears to take different shapes in the sky.

The Moon is an average distance from Earth of about 238,855 miles (384,400 km). It's still our nearest space neighbor, though. When we look at the night sky, we glimpse time passing each month as the Moon's appearance changes from one predictable shape to the next.

The size and shape of the Moon we see depends on how much of the sunlit side of the Moon is visible from Earth. These different shapes are called the phases of the Moon. There are eight phases. The full moon is one phase.

Halfway between one full moon and the following full moon is a phase called the new moon. This happens when the Moon is on the same side of Earth as is the Sun. At this time, the Sun shines on the side of the Moon facing away from Earth, with almost no light on the side facing Earth. That means the Moon appears completely dark and is invisible except through a telescope when viewed from Earth.

After the new moon, the Moon appears to get bigger every day, as it approaches the full moon phase. When the Moon is increasing in size, it is called a waxing moon. The waxing moon passes through three phases between the new moon and the full moon. These phases are

MAKING SENSE OF CYCLES

We normally associate the Moon with the sky at night, just as we associate the Sun with the daytime sky. Sometimes, however, we can see the Moon during the day. Why do you think this is so? Based on information in this chapter about the relationship in space between the Moon, the Sun, and Earth, explain how you think it's possible for us to see the Moon during the day.

called waxing crescent, first quarter, and waxing gibbous. A crescent moon appears as a sliver of the Moon. A gibbous moon is almost a full moon, with just a sliver of the Moon in darkness.

As the Moon appears to decrease in size from full moon to new moon, it is said to be waning. The three phases of the waning moon are waning gibbous, third quarter, and waning crescent.

Moon Morsels

• The Moon is about one-quarter of the size of Earth.
• It is about 238,900 miles (384,400 km) from Earth.
• The same side of the Moon always faces Earth.
• The Moon is covered with craters, ridges, mountain ranges, and flat plains. Its whole surface is coated with a thick layer of gray dust.

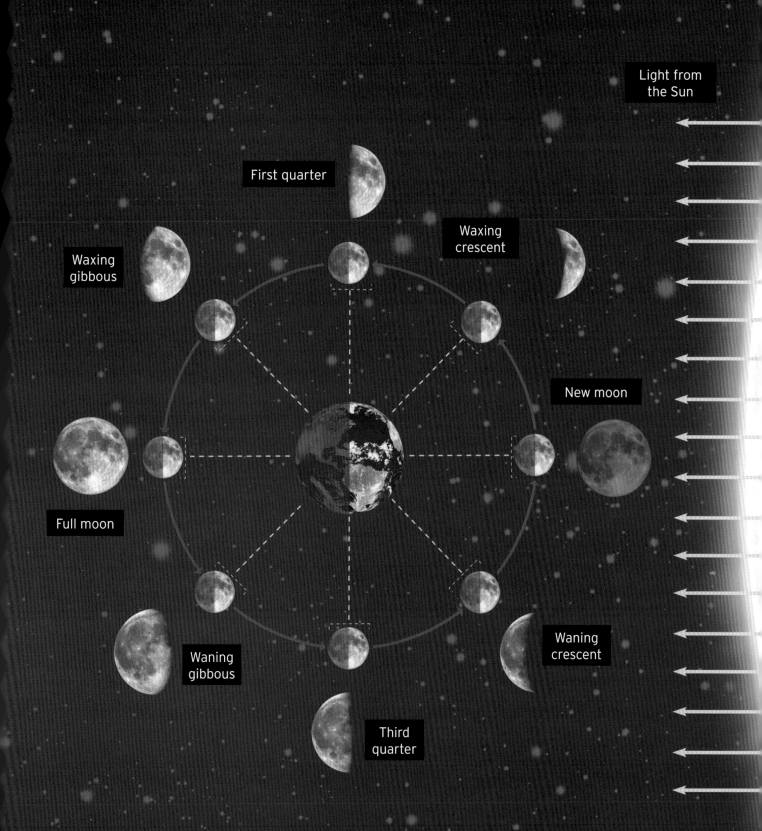

First quarter

Waxing crescent

Waxing gibbous

New moon

Full moon

Waning crescent

Waning gibbous

Third quarter

This diagram shows the Moon's phases as it makes one orbit of Earth. The inner ring of Moons in the diagram shows how the Sun's light hits the Moon. The outer ring of Moons shows how the Moon looks in the sky from here on Earth.

Rising and Falling

The Sun's gravity keeps Earth and all the other planets in our solar system in orbit around the Sun. Earth's gravity keeps the Moon in orbit around Earth. The Moon also has gravity. It's not as powerful as the gravity of the Sun or even Earth, but it does have an important effect on our planet.

About 70 percent of Earth is covered with oceans. It is primarily because of the pull of the Moon's gravity that those oceans have rising and falling tides.

The Moon's gravity tugs the surface of Earth slightly toward the Moon. Because Earth is covered with liquid water, and water moves fairly easily, the Moon's gravity pulls the water into bulges. The part of Earth facing the Moon experiences the greatest pull of gravity. Therefore, that part has the greatest bulge. As Earth rotates on its axis, this bulge of water, which is called a high tide, moves around the globe.

MAKING SENSE OF CYCLES

Our planet's daily rotation on its axis, its orbit around the Sun, and the Moon's orbit around Earth are cycles that involve the relationship of three important bodies in space—the Sun, Earth, and our Moon. All of these relationships involve cycles of various kinds. Think about similar cycles as they affect other objects in our solar system, such as asteroids, other planets, and their moons. How might these cycles be the same as those that we experience on Earth? How might they be different? Base your thinking on what you have read about these cycles and about other objects in space.

The Moon's gravity pulls everything on Earth toward it. The pull of the Moon's gravity on mountains and other solid objects is relatively slight. Water moves more easily, however, so we see the Moon's effect on the ocean as water levels rise and fall and the tide goes in and out.

The difference between high tide and low tide is called the tidal range. The highest tidal range in the world is in the Bay of Fundy, in a region of Canada known as Atlantic Canada. The tidal range there is about 50 feet (15 meters). That's about the height of a five-story building!

Most places on Earth have not one but two high tides each day. That's because the water on the side of Earth farthest from the Moon also experiences a tidal bulge. This tidal bulge on the "far side" of Earth from the Moon is due to several forces acting on our planet. One of them is called centrifugal force.

Imagine you are spinning on the spot, with both hands holding onto a rope tied to a bucket with water in it. You are spinning fast enough for the rope to extend away from you, and the bucket circles around with you. Centrifugal force is what makes the bucket pull at the end of the rope. It also makes the water push against the bottom of the bucket as the bucket flies in a circle around you.

In a similar way, as Earth is spinning on its axis, centrifugal force pushes ocean water away from Earth's surface. This creates a tidal bulge on the side of Earth that is farthest from the pull of the Moon. This would be the side where the pull of the Moon's gravity is weakest, and the effects of centrifugal force greatest. Also, the Moon's gravity is pulling at Earth and tugging the surface of that side of the planet away from the water and toward

This diagram shows the effect of the Moon's gravity on Earth's oceans. When any side of Earth is closest to the Moon (point A), the Moon's gravity causes the water to bulge, creating a high tide. At point C on the opposite side of Earth, the water also bulges. This happens because of several forces working on Earth and its water. One is centrifugal force, which pushes water away from Earth's surface. Another is the force of the Moon's gravity tugging at the Earth and pulling it away from the water on the "far side" of our planet. Points B and D are experiencing low tides.

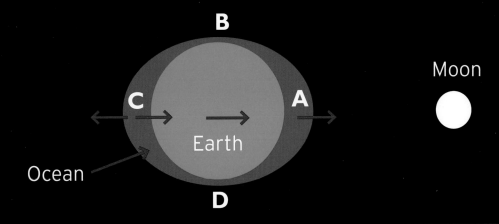

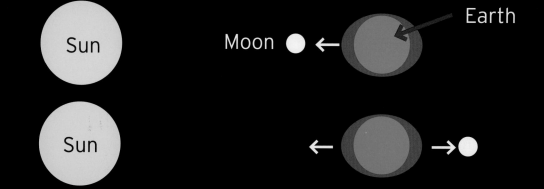

Sun

Moon ● ←

Earth

Sun

← →●

When the Sun, the Moon, and Earth are in line, Earth experiences its highest and lowest tides, as shown in this diagram. This is because both the Sun and the Moon are pulling on Earth's water.

Earth's center. This also has the effect of increasing the tidal bulge on the far side of Earth.

The Moon has the greatest impact on Earth's tides, but the Sun's gravity also affects them. The highest tides occur when the Sun and Moon are in line with each other, during the days of the full moon and the new moon.

Cycles of Time

Before the invention of calendars and clocks, ancient peoples looked to the sky to measure the passing of time. They realized that the rising and setting of the Sun was a pattern that happened over and over again. They also noticed that even though the look, or phases, of the Moon changed from day to day, the pattern of the Moon's phases regularly repeated itself. Ancient peoples also saw that the Sun followed a path through the stars in the sky, eventually returning to the point where they believed it had started.

These repeating cycles became the basis for calendars. The time between sunrises came to be known as a day. The time between full moons came to be known as a month. And the time it took for the Sun, to make its full journey through the stars, was known as a year.

Early calendars were based on the lunar month, or 29.5 days. The problem was that the solar year, the Sun's cycle, was 365+ days. A solar year didn't divide into an even number of lunar months. Twelve lunar months total only 354 days, while 13 lunar months total 383+ days.

To account for this variation, some early calendars alternated between 12-month years and 13-month years. Others alternated between 29-day and 30-day months, with an added

Newgrange is a temple that was built more than 5,000 years ago in Ireland. Beneath its vast mound (inset below) is a chamber and passageway, shown here. Ancient peoples built this structure with such precision that it catches the Sun's light in a small opening, called a "roof-box," in December, on the shortest days of the year. At around 9:00 A.M. on those days, a beam of light enters through the roof-box, moves down the passageway, and illuminates the entire passage and chamber for exactly 17 minutes. One of the purposes for this building and its roof-box was probably to signal the end of the longest nights of the year and mark the beginning of the new year. For thousands of years, people standing in the chamber have been able to use the structure and the Sun to tell the time with as much accuracy as any modern-day clock or computer.

month every few years to keep the months and seasons in line. Some calendars used 12 lunar months and just ignored the extra 11 days!

The calendar we use today is based on the Julian calendar. This calendar gets its name from the fact that it was created 2,500 years ago during the reign of Julius Caesar. In that calendar, every month had 30 or 31 days. February usually had 29 days, with 30 days every fourth year.

After about 1,500 years of using this system, though, the calendar year and the true solar year no longer matched up. They were off by about ten days! The calendar was shifted, to make up the ten days and February became a 28-day month (with 29 days every fourth year, which we called a "leap year") from then on. This calendar is the one most countries use today. It is called the Gregorian calendar. Some cultures still use the Julian calendar. It is currently about 13 days behind the Gregorian calendar.

MAKING SENSE OF CYCLES

Our Moon is, in many ways, Earth's "partner" in space. In addition to being a source of inspiration for songwriters and poets for thousands of years, the Moon plays an important role in the physical life of our planet. Think of the ways that the Moon affects Earth. Now imagine Earth without its Moon. What kinds of things would change? How would life be different? In what ways do you think things might not be affected at all? Use information from this book to help explain your thinking.

Lunar Celebrations

The Moon is still used as a guide for many cultural festivals. Jewish and Islamic holy days and celebrations are based on a historic lunar calendar, as is the date of Easter in the Christian calendar. Interestingly, Western Christians use the Gregorian calendar (the calendar that most countries use for business and daily life), while Eastern Orthodox Christians use the Julian calendar. That means Easter happens on different days for these different groups. Even though the official calendar of China is the Gregorian calendar, some festivals, such as Chinese New Year, are still based on a lunar calendar.

This photograph taken by astronaut Neil Armstrong shows Buzz Aldrin standing on the Moon. A tiny portion of the leg of the landing module, Eagle, can be seen lower right. Armstrong is also visible, reflected in the visor of Aldrin's helmet.

Footsteps on the Moon

On July 21, 1969, U.S. astronaut Neil Armstrong made history when he stepped onto the surface of the Moon. He was the first person ever to do that! Fellow astronaut Buzz Aldrin joined him a few minutes later, while crewmate Michael Collins orbited above the lunar surface in the command spacecraft. Armstrong and Aldrin spent 21 and a half hours on the Moon, mostly inside their spacecraft. They walked on the Moon for about two and a half hours.

Over the next three years, 10 more U.S. astronauts walked on the Moon. These 12 astronauts are the only people who have ever set foot on the Moon.

Nobody has been there since 1972, mostly because of budget cuts, political hurdles, and an emphasis on unmanned missions farther out in space. A number of countries, including the United States, Russia, China, and India, are considering future missions to the Moon.

CHAPTER 5

Weather Report

Let's say you get up one morning, and you see that the Sun is out. You might plan for a lovely, sunny day. By the afternoon, though, it has turned rainy and chilly. The next day, it's snowing. Weird, you might think. Sometimes, it appears as if the weather makes no sense, that it's completely random. In fact, though, there are systems—and cycles—at work in the world that drive weather patterns. And even though the weather may seem random, most of what we experience in weather is part of larger cycles and patterns that we can understand and even predict. We know, for example, that in most parts of the United States and Canada, summers are warm (or hot) and winters are cool (or cold!). That's a weather cycle that repeats year after year. The heat from the Sun, along with Earth's tilt, spin, and orbit, are what make the world's weather cycles go 'round.

The Air Out There

Surrounding Earth is a blanket of gases called the atmosphere. The atmosphere controls temperatures on Earth. It protects us from burning up in the heat of the Sun during the day, and it holds warmth around us at night. The oxygen in the atmosphere allows us to breathe. The carbon dioxide in the atmosphere keeps plants alive. The atmosphere is also where weather happens.

This photo of Earth's atmosphere (the thick blue strip) was taken by a camera aboard the International Space Station.

The Layers of Earth's Atmosphere

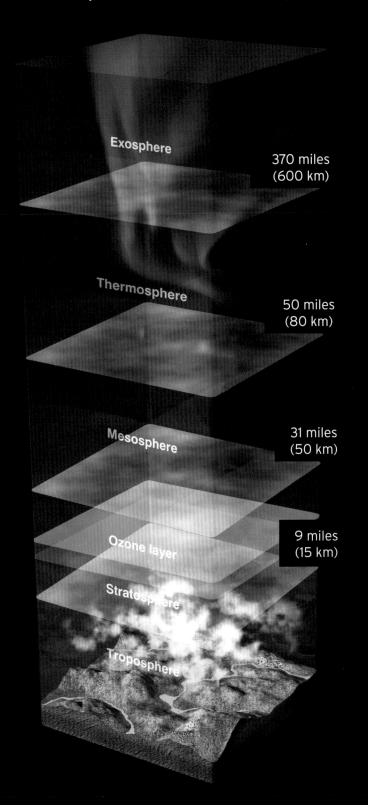

Exosphere — 370 miles (600 km)

Thermosphere — 50 miles (80 km)

Mesosphere — 31 miles (50 km)

Ozone layer — 9 miles (15 km)

Stratosphere

Troposphere

The troposphere, stratosphere, mesosphere, and thermosphere are the main layers that make up Earth's atmosphere. Above these layers is the exosphere, the region where the atmosphere becomes much thinner and eventually merges with outer space. The altitude of each layer varies around the planet, and the heights shown in this diagram show comparative altitudes. The diagram also shows the ozone layer (see chapter 6).

Most scientists divide Earth's atmosphere into five different regions or layers. The innermost layer is called the troposphere. This is where all weather systems occur. The troposphere starts at the planet's surface and goes 7–10 miles (11–16 km) into the sky, depending on where on Earth you are.

If you were flying in a jetliner, you'd probably be in the lower regions of the next layer of atmosphere, the stratosphere, which is where most passenger planes fly. If you were at an altitude of about 35,000 feet (10,000 m), and you looked out the window, you would be able to look *down* at the thick, dense clouds that usually produce precipitation. That's because these clouds are part of weather, which happens in the troposphere below.

The air in the troposphere is constantly on the move, heating up, cooling down, and swirling around. All this activity, and such weather conditions as wind, rain, snow, and clouds, are the result of the atmosphere responding to the uneven ways in which Earth is heated by the Sun.

We know that Earth is tilted, making the angle of sunlight on some parts of the planet more direct, or focused, than on others. Also, the altitude, or height, of some features like mountains account for differences in how parts of our planet are heated. That means some places—regions near the equator,

From the window of a jetliner you can see Earth's surface far below you and you look out into Earth's atmosphere. As your plane climbs, you might travel from the troposphere up into the stratosphere. Then, you get the chance to be above the weather instead of beneath it!

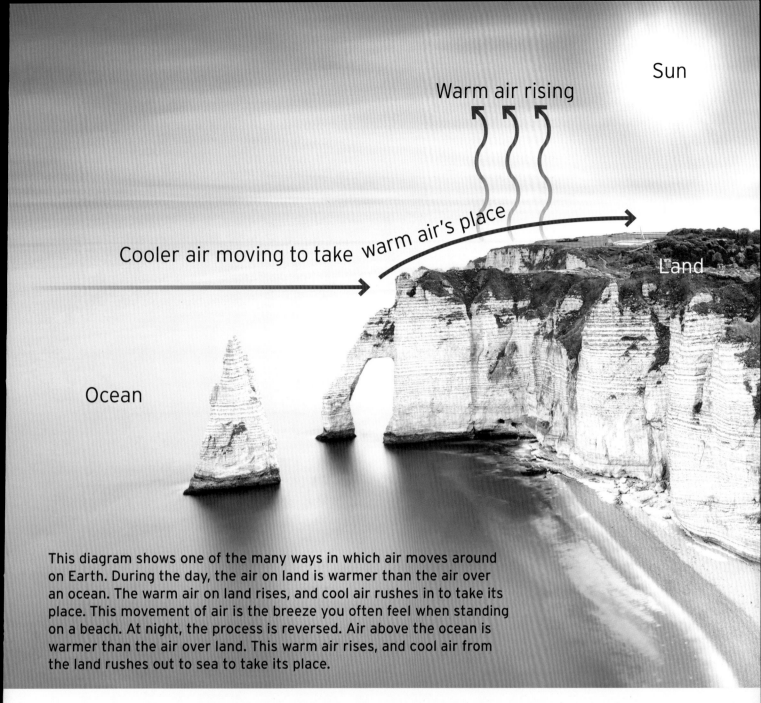

Sun

Warm air rising

Cooler air moving to take warm air's place

Land

Ocean

This diagram shows one of the many ways in which air moves around on Earth. During the day, the air on land is warmer than the air over an ocean. The warm air on land rises, and cool air rushes in to take its place. This movement of air is the breeze you often feel when standing on a beach. At night, the process is reversed. Air above the ocean is warmer than the air over land. This warm air rises, and cool air from the land rushes out to sea to take its place.

for example—are warmer than others. Warm air is less dense than cold air. Gravity has more "pull" on colder, more dense air. This means that warm air tends to rise, creating air **currents** that move up into the atmosphere. These rising air currents cause rain-producing **cumulus clouds** and thunderstorms. When warm air rises, cooler air moves in to replace it. The cooler air then warms up, rises, and makes room for more cool air.

In addition to moving up and down (vertically), warm air and cool air also move across the surface of the planet (horizontally). This movement is caused by differences in temperature on Earth's surface between the poles and regions closer to the equator. These temperature differences cause other changes in the atmosphere, such as a change in air pressure, which lead to the movement of air that we know as wind!

Cycles on a Global Scale

Individual wind cycles are part of larger global airflow cycles that continually move warm air from the equator to Earth's polar regions and back again.

Global currents called jet streams also circle the globe in fast-moving, curvy, zigzagging pathways. Jet streams can be thousands of miles long, hundreds of miles wide, and several miles thick. Jet streams move from west to east around the planet, carrying weather systems with them. They occur at the level of the atmosphere where the troposphere and stratosphere meet. At this level, there is an extreme temperature change. Jet streams may split into two or more parts, combine

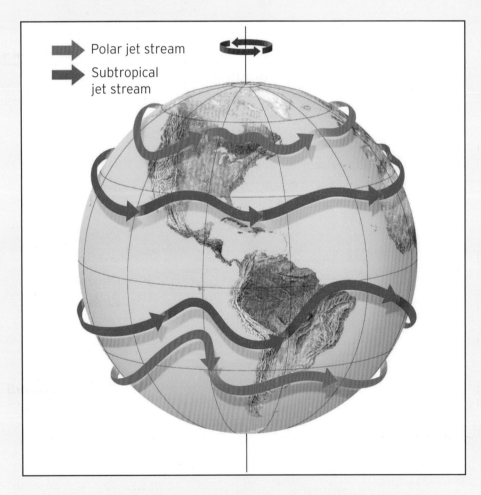

Polar jet stream

Subtropical jet stream

This artwork shows the pathways of the jet streams as they move west to east around Earth. Jet streams move at more than 200 miles per hour (322 kmh). Planes often fly in the same direction as jet streams and use these fast-moving currents to help them fly faster.

into one stream, or flow in various directions within the main stream.

The direction of air currents is also affected by the rotation of our planet. As Earth spins, air currents in the northern hemisphere are deflected to the right, or clockwise. Air currents in the southern hemisphere are deflected to the left, or counterclockwise.

Air in our atmosphere also contains water vapor, which is water in its gaseous state. Warmer air holds more water than cooler air. When warm air rises, it takes this water vapor with it. The air cools as it rises. Eventually, it reaches a temperature at which the water vapor in the air **condenses** into tiny droplets of liquid water. The vapor requires a surface on which it may condense into a liquid. This surface may be in the form of dust, salt, or other particles in the air. When enough of these droplets gather together, they form clouds.

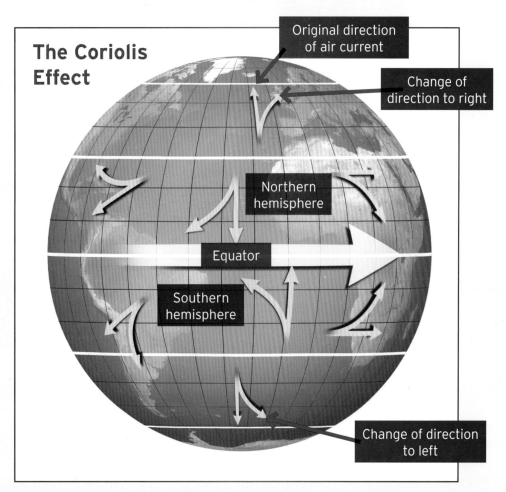

The Coriolis Effect

Original direction of air current

Change of direction to right

Northern hemisphere

Equator

Southern hemisphere

Change of direction to left

The effect of Earth's rotation on air currents is called the Coriolis Effect. It is named after Gustave Coriolis, the French scientist who first described the effect. This diagram shows straight arrows, which illustrate the initial directions of air currents' movements. In the northern hemisphere, the air currents are then deflected off to the right by the Coriolis Effect. In the southern hemisphere, the air currents move off to the left.

Eventually, the drops of water become too heavy to stay in the clouds. Gravity pulls them toward Earth, and they fall as rain. If the temperature in the cloud is below freezing, the vapor in the air forms ice crystals, instead of water droplets.

These tiny ice crystals bond together to form larger crystals. When these crystals become too heavy to stay in a cloud, they fall as snow.

This movement of water between its liquid, solid, and gaseous states is part of what we call the water cycle.

The Water Cycle

Water droplets gather together and form rain clouds. In very cold air, water drops may freeze and form snow.

Water vapor rises high into the atmosphere, where cold temperatures cause it to condense and form water droplets.

Rain and snow fall from clouds back to Earth.

Water on Earth is warmed by the Sun, evaporates, and becomes a gas called water vapor.

Rainwater and melted snow run into rivers, which eventually run into the ocean.

The water cycle affects us every day whenever we drink water, take a shower, or dress for a rainy or snowy day. But it also happens on a global scale. Thanks to the movement of wind currents in the atmosphere, water that **evaporates** in the Great Lakes might end up falling as rain over a farm in Mexico!

Sometimes, especially in hot tropical zones, warm air and cool air swirl around so quickly that the wind becomes dangerously powerful. This can lead to hurricanes, tornadoes, and electrically charged thunderstorms.

The better scientists understand all the cycles that contribute to short-term weather conditions, the better they can predict the weather systems that are coming our way. These predictions, or forecasts, can help us decide whether we should plan for a sunny day at the beach, spend a rainy day playing indoor games, or escape to a safe place during a hurricane.

Short-Term and Long-Term

Weather and climate are related, but they are not the same thing. Weather is what you see outside at a particular moment in time in a particular place. If you look out the window and see that it's cloudy and raining, that is the weather on that day.

This photograph shows Hurricane Frances in the Atlantic Ocean in August 2004. It was taken by Mike Finke, an astronaut aboard the International Space Station. Hurricanes may grow to be 600 miles (966 km) wide.

At any one time, there are around 2,000 thunderstorms happening on Earth.

Predictable in its Unpredictability

You may have heard the term *El Niño* (pronounced "el-NEEN-yoh"). El Niño is a climate pattern—sort of. It happens when the Pacific Ocean off the west coast of South America becomes unusually warm. El Niño affects ocean temperatures, ocean currents, and weather patterns around the world. For example, on the West Coast of Canada and the United States, El Niño brings more rain and warmer temperatures than usual. *El Niño*, which means "the boy" in Spanish, happens every two to seven years, but not at regular intervals. Scientists have not yet been able to predict accurately when it will occur. A recent El Niño happened in 2010.

Spring: The weather is warm and sunny, and there may be rain. Many animals have their young.

Summer: The weather is hot, and often there is little rain. People wear lightweight clothes and spend lots of time outdoors.

Many parts of the world have a temperate climate, where it's possible to see and feel the weather changing as the seasons change.

Winter: The temperature is cold. People wear hats, boots, and thick clothing to protect themselves from snow and icy winds.

Fall: The temperature is much cooler than summer. There is often rain. People wrap up warm to spend time outside.

Climate refers to the average weather pattern of a place over a long period of time. For example, if it is cold and snowy every January over a 30-year period in cities like Buffalo, Chicago, Milwaukee, and Toronto, we could safely say that those cities are cold and snowy in January. That describes the climate, or long-term weather pattern, of the city.

Some climate patterns span thousands of years. An ice age is an example of such a pattern. Earth has experienced at least five ice ages during the past three billion years. An ice age happens when Earth's overall temperature drops by 10°-40°F (5°-20°C). At these times, parts of the planet are covered with thick sheets of ice, or glaciers. Within an ice age, temperatures fluctuate, or vary. We are actually in an ice age right now—just a warmer part of an ice age.

Ice ages may be caused by slight changes in Earth's orbit around the Sun, or a shift in the tilt of Earth on its axis. Ocean currents and the amount of carbon dioxide in the atmosphere also affect long-term climate. The more carbon dioxide in the air, the warmer the climate becomes.

It may be impossible for human activity to change the orbit of Earth or the Moon, or the tilt of Earth on its axis. Still, our activities can have an impact on climate and weather patterns.

Musk oxen survive in the extreme icy temperatures of the Canadian Arctic as they have for thousands of years. During the coldest times in Earth's ice ages, many parts of the world were covered with giant fields of ice. In fact, 20,000 years ago, much of Canada and the northern United States would have looked just like this picture!

CHAPTER 6

Changing Systems

Scientists aren't sure exactly what effect human activities will have on Earth's climate cycles thousands of years from now. They do, however, have some ideas about the effect of our actions on our planet now and in the not-so-distant future. Right now, for example, some human activities are harming the atmosphere. This in turn can harm life on Earth and disrupt weather cycles, which will have an effect on our planet's climate.

Stressing Out the Atmosphere

In today's world, people depend on **fossil fuels**, such as coal, oil, and natural gas. When they burn, these fuels release harmful gases into our air. The more fossil fuels we burn, the more of these gases enter the atmosphere.

Earth's atmosphere has always contained certain amounts of these gases. They keep the planet warm and able to support life. In recent years, though, the amount of these gases in our atmosphere has increased dramatically, causing problems for the planet.

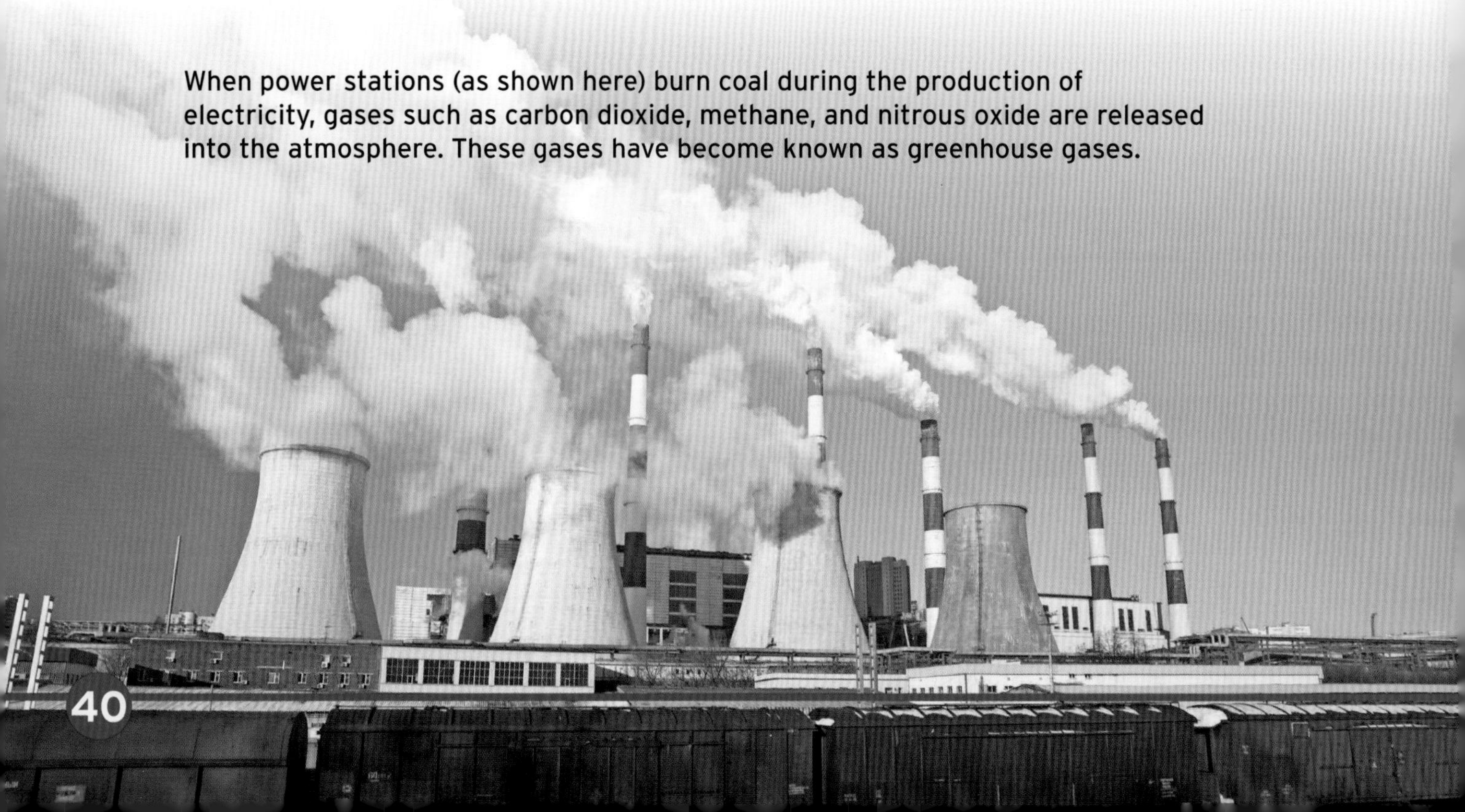

When power stations (as shown here) burn coal during the production of electricity, gases such as carbon dioxide, methane, and nitrous oxide are released into the atmosphere. These gases have become known as greenhouse gases.

When the concentration of these gases increases, Earth's atmosphere starts to act like a greenhouse, trapping more and more of the Sun's heat. Just like the air in a garden greenhouse, the temperature inside our atmosphere becomes warmer than it might otherwise be. This pattern of climate change is called **global warming**, and the gases are called **greenhouse gases**.

Warmer temperatures mean glaciers and Arctic ice will melt, and ocean levels will rise. Higher temperatures may also lead to droughts, or dry spells. Without enough rain, crops won't grow properly. Rising global temperatures also lead to unusual weather patterns and increasingly severe natural disasters such as hurricanes, wildfires, and drought. Other potential impacts of climate change include seasons changing at slightly different times of year, animals becoming endangered or even extinct because of changes to their habitat, and a decreasing supply of fresh water.

A Hole in the Sky

Within the stratosphere is a layer of gas called **ozone**. The ozone layer is an important part of the atmosphere because it prevents harmful ultraviolet (UV) radiation from the Sun from reaching Earth. UV rays can cause sunburn on humans and other mammals. They can also cause skin cancer.

In the 1980s, scientists discovered that this protective ozone layer around Earth was getting thinner. It continues to thin today because of certain chemicals used on Earth. These chemicals get into the atmosphere and react with ozone to produce other compounds, removing ozone from the atmosphere.

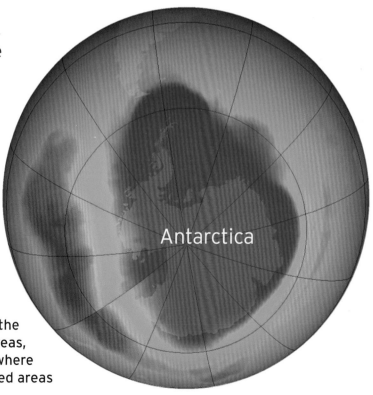

Antarctica

This view of ozone in the atmosphere over the South Pole in September 2014 has been colored on a computer to show the amounts of ozone. The purple and blue areas, which cover nearly all of Antarctica, are where there is the least ozone. The yellow and red areas show where there is the most ozone.

Because of wind and temperature patterns, the ozone layer above the South Pole gets so thin every spring that it is called an ozone hole. It's not actually a hole, but it is a dangerously thin layer of ozone.

The Sun's energy feels hotter where the ozone layer is reduced. That's because more of those harmful UV rays reach Earth's surface. In addition to threatening the health of animals, excess UV rays can throw off natural plant growth cycles.

Harnessing Earth's Cycles

For years, scientists and engineers have been working to find ways to reduce humans' use of fossil fuels. That will help reduce the production of greenhouse gases. This, in turn, will help lessen the severity of Earth's weather patterns and keep the ozone layer intact.

Some researchers are developing electric cars, airplanes powered by **biofuels** made from algae and plant

MAKING SENSE OF CYCLES

Scientists cannot predict with absolute certainty what Earth will be like thousands of years from now. We do know a lot about conditions on our planet today and in recent years, however. And based on what we know now, we can observe cycles and patterns that might affect the future of our planet. How might things happening now on our planet, including the atmosphere and bodies of water, affect the future of Earth hundreds of years from now? Use information you have read in this book and examples you can think of in your own life and from other sources to explain your answer.

By studying Earth's wind patterns, scientists can determine where best to place **wind turbines**, or generators, to capture this natural airflow. **Wind farms** are built on land and offshore. This wind farm is in the Baltic Sea off the coast of Copenhagen, Denmark.

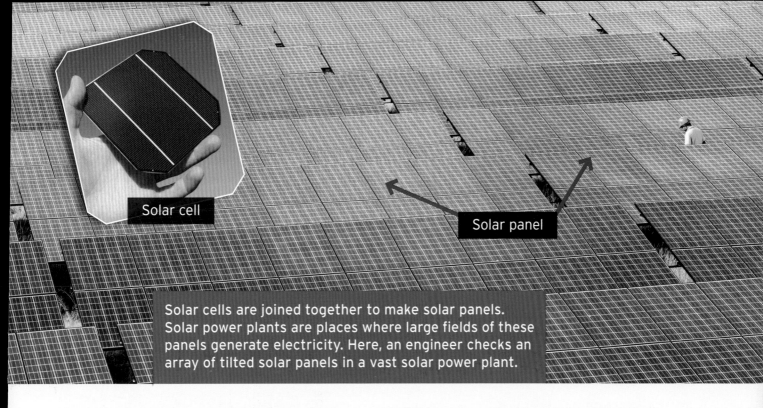

Solar cell

Solar panel

Solar cells are joined together to make solar panels. Solar power plants are places where large fields of these panels generate electricity. Here, an engineer checks an array of tilted solar panels in a vast solar power plant.

materials, and trains that are pulled along their tracks by magnetic forces. Engineers are finding new ways to build homes and factories that use less energy. Certain manufacturers are developing products made from recycled materials. This cuts down on manufacturing that uses fossil fuel-based resources.

Meanwhile, other researchers are looking to the cycles of the Moon, Earth, and Sun for help in reducing our dependence on fossil fuels. We know, for example, that the Moon's gravity drives the tides in Earth's oceans. Engineers are designing devices that can tap into tidal power, the natural energy of rising and falling water in coastal areas, to generate electricity.

Wind is another natural, **renewable energy source**. It has been used

by sailors for hundreds of years to power boats. Windmills originally harnessed the wind to mill, or grind, grains. Now they are used to produce electricity for homes, businesses, and towns.

Then there's the Sun and all its power. The energy contained in the sunlight that reaches Earth's surface in just one hour could meet the world's energy demands for an entire year! We're not at that point yet, but engineers have designed **solar cells** that can capture some of the energy from the Sun's rays and convert it to electricity.

The more we understand about the Sun, the Moon, and Earth's cycles, the more we can use the natural energy they produce. One day, you may become one of the scientists or engineers who help harness new, natural energy sources!

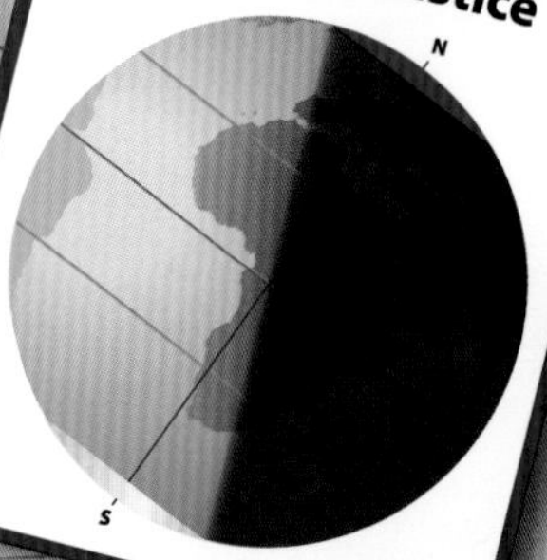

Solstice Sunlight

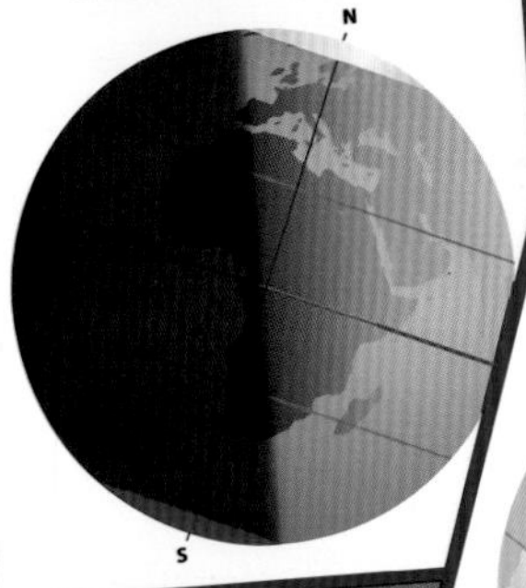

You have learned that as Earth rotates on its axis and orbits the Sun, the path of the Sun's light moves across the surface of the planet. Every day, the amount of sunlight is different than it was on the previous day. In the northern hemisphere, the longest day of the year occurs on the summer solstice, and the shortest day is on the winter solstice. These days are on or close to June 21 (summer) and December 21 (winter).

On the days when the length of daylight is either the longest or the shortest of the year, does location affect how much daylight a place receives?

In this activity, you will use the Internet to find out the length of daylight in several cities and towns on the same two days of the year–December 21 and June 21. As you record your findings, observe the differences between each place, and compare their locations on a map to see if there is a pattern that might explain any differences or similarities in length of daylight.

summer solstice

winter solstice

You Will Need

- Computer with access to an Internet search engine, such as Google
- Notebook or pad of paper and pen or pencil

Instructions

1 In your notebook, write down the following place names for easy reference, as shown here.

City	State/Territory	Country
Resolute Bay	Nunavut	Canada
Baker Lake	Nunavut	Canada
Thompson	Manitoba	Canada
Winnipeg	Manitoba	Canada
Milwaukee	Wisconsin	United States
Kansas City	Missouri	United States
San Antonio	Texas	United States
Mexico City	Federal District	Mexico

Hours of daylight on June 21, 20 - -

City	Hours	Minutes
Resolute Bay	21	03
Baker Lake	17	28
Mexico City		

2 Then create two charts in your notebook, one for December 21 and one for June 21, in which to record data. Use this chart as a model to get started.

3 Find websites online that show the length of daylight for any place on the globe. Hint: Use "length of daylight" for the keyword window in your search engine. When you reach a site, enter the exact date you are looking for.

Here is a site you might check out:

http://www.solartopo.com/daylength.htm

4 In your notebook, record the hours and minutes of daylight for each location and date. You may also make notes about any similarities or differences in the locations of these places based on this map.

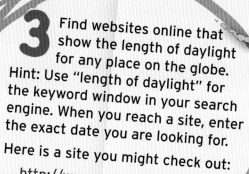

Resolute Bay

Baker Lake

Thompson

Winnipeg

Kansas City

Milwaukee

San Antonio

Mexico City

The Challenge

When you have completed your charts, look them over carefully for patterns, similarities, and differences. Then present your data to others and discuss:

- Which locations have the longest and shortest days, and what their location might have to do with the amount of daylight they receive.
- Which locations have the least difference between longest and shortest days, and what their location might have to do with this.
- What patterns you see as you move south from Resolute Bay.
- What predictions you might make about the length of daylight at a location south of Mexico City.
- Try the same activity for cities or towns of your own choosing and see what kinds of patterns, if any, you can detect in the results.

air pressure The force exerted on a surface by the weight of air above it. The more densely packed the molecules in the atmosphere are, the more it weighs, and the higher the air pressure is. Air pressure is often associated with weather patterns and systems

asteroid A rocky body that orbits the Sun and may range in size from a particle of dust to hundreds of miles wide

atmosphere The layer of gases surrounding Earth

axis An imaginary line around which an object in space rotates, or spins

biofuel A renewable fuel made from living matter, including algae and plant sources, such as corn

climate zones Areas of Earth that are defined by their annual weather conditions, including average temperatures and average amount of rainfall

condense To convert, or change, a substance from a gaseous state to a liquid state. When water vapor condenses, it becomes liquid water

cumulus cloud A low-altitude cloud forming rounded masses piled upon one another. Cumulus clouds rarely produce precipitation, but they can develop into rain-producing clouds

current A body of air or water moving in a specific direction, usually through a surrounding body in which there is less movement

evaporate To convert to a gaseous state. For example, when water evaporates, it becomes water vapor

fossil fuel A fuel source that began as organisms or plant material buried deep beneath Earth's surface underwent decomposition and other natural processes, usually over periods of millions of years, and were eventually converted to oil, coal, or natural gas

global warming The gradual increase in the temperature of Earth's atmosphere due to the increased levels of greenhouse gases

greenhouse gases Gases, including carbon dioxide, methane, and ozone, that contribute to the warming of Earth's temperatures

hemisphere Half of the Earth as divided into either northern and southern hemispheres by the equator or eastern and western hemispheres by an imaginary line passing through the poles

Kuiper Belt A region of the solar system beyond the orbit of Neptune, believed to contain millions of asteroids, comets, and other small bodies made mostly of ice

lunar month The period from one full moon to the next full moon, about 29.5 days

Oort Cloud A spherical region in space beyond the Kuiper Belt that is believed to be home to trillions of comets and other small rocky and icy bodies

ozone An unstable form of oxygen made from three oxygen atoms and formed by electrical discharges or ultraviolet light

photosynthesis A process by which plants convert carbon dioxide, water, and sunlight into oxygen and sugars

polar zone A climate zone around the North or South Poles

renewable energy source A resource that will never run out, such as the energy from wind, water, or the Sun

solar cell A device, often in the form of a flat panel, designed to capture energy from the Sun and convert it into electricity

temperate zone Each of the two climate zones between the polar zones and the tropical zone. Most places in the temperate zones experiences four distinct seasons

tropical zone The climate zone closest to the equator, between the equator and the temperate zones

wind farm An area with energy-producing windmills or wind turbines

wind turbine A machine with a large wheel, similar to the vanes on a windmill, that spins and generates power when the wind strikes it

BOOKS

Cosgrove, Brian. *Eyewitness: Weather* (DK Eyewitness Books). New York: DK Publishing, 2007.

Mitton, Jacqueline. *Eyewitness: Moon.* (DK Eyewitness Books). New York: DK Publishing, 2009.

Oxlade, Chris. *Earth and Its Moon* (Earth and Space). New York: Rosen Publishing Group, 2008.

WEBSITES

www.weatherwizkids.com/weather-wind.htm
Learn all about weather systems on this site, called *Weather Wiz Kids*. This particular page is all about wind and how warm and cool air interact to make wind. From here, you can link to pages about climate, clouds, rain, and storms.

space-facts.com/
This is a cool website with sections devoted to Moon Facts, Earth Facts, Sun Facts, Asteroid Facts, and more! It features photos and factoids about space.

www.kids.esdb.bg/ocean.html
www.kids.esdb.bg/solar.html
www.kids.esdb.bg/wind.html
These three sites on the *Kids & Energy* website link to information about three different kinds of renewable energy–tidal, solar, and wind.

education.nationalgeographic.com/education/encyclopedia/tide/?ar_a=1
Everything you need to know about tides is on this National Geographic webpage. It explains the relationship between the Moon, the Sun, and tides in simple terms–but if you want more detail, it's there too! There are also some excellent photos and graphics.

INDEX

ABOUT THE AUTHOR

Diane Dakers was born and raised in Toronto, and now lives in Victoria, British Columbia, Canada. A newspaper, TV, and radio journalist since 1991, she lives in a place where she witnesses the effects of Earth, Sun, and Moon cycles in action—ocean tides, long summer days, short winter days, and four distinct seasons.